Taylor's Pocket Guide to

Ground Covers for Shade

D0311419

Taylor's Pocket Guide to

Ground Covers
for Shade

ANN REILLY
Consulting Editor

A Chanticleer Press Edition

Houghton Mifflin Company

Boston

Based on Taylor's Encyclopedia of Gardening, Fourth Edition,
Copyright © 1961 by Norman Taylor,
revised and edited by
Gordon P. DeWolf, Jr.

Prepared and produced by Chanticleer Press, New York
Typeset by Dix Type, Inc., Syracuse, New York
Printed and bound by
Dai Nippon, Tokyo, Japan

Library of Congress Catalog Card Number: 89-85029
ISBN: 0-395-52248-X

DNP   10   9   8   7   6   5   4   3   2   1

CONTENTS

GARDENING WITH
GROUND COVERS FOR SHADE

BEGINNING GARDENERS often think of shade as a problem spot, lacking color, where few plants will grow. Nothing could be further from the truth. This book presents a wide variety of ground covers that thrive in different shady situations. You can use them to line a walkway on the north side of the house, to unify shrub borders that create heavy shade, to carpet the ground beneath tall trees where a lawn won't grow, or to bring color to a woodland garden.

What Is a Ground Cover?

Ground covers are a diverse group of annual and perennial plants. They may be herbaceous plants, dying down in winter, woody vines, or low-growing shrubs. An important part of any garden, ground covers unite the house with other elements in the landscape—trees, shrubs, walkways, patios, and lawns. If carefully chosen and creatively used, these practical plants can add considerable interest to those parts of your garden that do not receive sun most of the day.

A large and varied assortment of ground covers will flourish in shady places. Some are evergreen, while others are deciduous, losing their leaves in winter; some have tenacious roots that help prevent soil erosion; and some can thrive in poor soil where other plants will not grow well. Shade-loving ground covers are both practical and attractive, offering a wide range of foliage and flowers.

Types of Ground Covers

The ground covers listed in this book are herbaceous perennials, vines, and low-growing shrubs. An herbaceous perennial is a plant that grows and flowers each year, dies to the ground in winter, and grows again the following spring. Where a perennial is not winter hardy, it may be planted in early spring and grown as an annual—a plant that grows, flowers, sets seed, and dies in one growing season. There are no true annuals listed in this book, but tender perennials can be used as annual ground covers for temporary landscapes or to fill in the areas between small, young plants until the permanent ground cover matures.

Vines are woody perennials, with long, pliable stems, which creep along the ground as they grow. The stems of many vines root as the plants grow, thus making a tight, dense cover. Vines may lose their leaves in winter, but the stems usually do not die back. Shrubs are also woody plants whose stems remain evident in winter. Low-growing, spreading shrubs make excellent ground covers.

Deciduous or Evergreen?

A woody plant may be either deciduous or evergreen; if its leaves drop in the fall, it is deciduous. Evergreens, which may be broad-leaved or needle-leaved, retain some or all of their foliage during the winter dormancy. The leaves of most evergreens remain green, but those of a few turn color in fall.

Many evergreens shed some of their older foliage in the spring when new growth starts.

Whether you plant evergreen or deciduous ground covers depends on personal preference and the area in the garden that you are planting. A large, bare stretch that is unattractive in winter looks best covered with an evergreen plant. A deciduous ground cover is perfectly acceptable under deciduous trees and shrubs, while an evergreen would work best under an evergreen foundation planting.

How Ground Covers Spread

It is a plant's spreading growth habit that makes it valuable as a ground cover. Plants spread in different ways. The low-growing shrubs used for ground covers have branches that extend out to the sides; the branches of some root where they touch the ground. Other shrubs spread in diameter by producing suckers, which are new stems, at the base of the plant. Vining plants send out long runners, which usually root as they creep along the ground. Some ground covers spread by rhizomes or stolons, which are stems or roots that spread underground or at ground level, and send up new erect stems as they grow. The flowers of some ground covers drop seeds that easily self-sow, so the planting increases rapidly as new plants grow up.

First Steps Toward Planting

Many of the ground covers in this book are excellent choices for problem spots; others will simply add color and beauty to your landscape as they tie different elements together.

The ground covers that you choose must be able to survive in your garden, whether it is hot or cold, dry or wet. Some ground covers are so rugged they will grow almost anywhere; others have very specific growing needs. Before you begin, assess your needs and environmental conditions—then you can choose ground covers that will thrive in your garden.

How Much Shade?

The ground covers discussed in this book are those that grow best in some degree of shade. The density of shade varies with the time of day, the time of year, and the source of the shade. Shadows cast by buildings are heavier than those cast by trees, because some sunlight always filters through leaves. Trees in full leaf cast more shade than the same trees in early spring. There is more daylight during summer in the North than in the South, so there is more light, even in shaded gardens.

The term "light shade" is applied to situations with up to six hours of sunlight each day, or lightly dappled shade cast all day by trees and shrubs. "Partial shade" means about four hours of sun, or more heavily dappled shade all day. "Full shade" means less than four hours of sunlight daily, or very heavily dappled shade from trees and shrubs.

All plants—even those that flourish in shade—benefit from some morning sun, which dries off the foliage and reduces the chance of disease. Afternoon sun, however, is too strong for most plants, especially shade-loving plants. No ground cover will survive in dense shade with no direct light at all. If the shade cast by trees is too dense, you can thin out some of the upper branches or remove some of the lower branches to let more light through. Some of the ground covers suitable for shade will also grow in full sun, and some prefer sun in northern regions where summers are cool, humid, or moist.

Hardiness

One of the first things you should consider when you choose ground covers is plant hardiness. Hardiness is the measure of a plant's fitness to survive in a particular climate. The U.S. Department of Agriculture has devised a hardiness zone map (see pages 106–107) that divides North America into ten climatic zones based on minimum temperatures in winter. Zone 1 is the coldest, with winter lows of −50° F, and zone 10 is the warmest, with minimums of 30° F.

Find your area on the map and determine your hardiness zone. You will be able to grow most plants that are hardy to your zone and any of the colder zones. If a plant is hardy to zone 5, it will live over winter in zones 10 through 5, but will probably not survive the colder winters in zones 4 through 1.

Keep in mind that the lines on the map and the minimum temperatures given are averages. There are a number of factors that may affect a plant's hardiness. A colder-than-average winter could damage plants that are normally hardy. High altitude, rainfall, and soil conditions can also influence a plant's ability to survive.

Microclimates

Within each zone there are areas with conditions that differ from those in the rest of the zone. These areas, which can be as large as a city or as small as a backyard garden, are called microclimates. If your garden is surrounded by a wall, fence, or hedge, it may be warmer than the rest of your zone. Temperatures are usually lower, however, on the north side of a house or building and at the bottom of a hill.

Before you begin experimenting with microclimates, stick with plants that you know are hardy to your zone. As they grow, you will come to know your garden and its variations; you can then test plants in small areas before you try to cover large expanses with them.

Garden Soil

Most ground covers grow best in soil that has good drainage (that doesn't hold too much water). The preference for dry or moist, rich or poor soil varies greatly from plant to plant. The plant descriptions indicate the type of soil in which a particular plant grows best. This does not mean that the plant will grow in that type of soil only; rather, those are the conditions for optimum growth. If your soil is not ideal, don't despair— you can improve it somewhat or you can choose plants that will thrive in your soil conditions.

Because they naturally grow in a woodland habitat, many ground covers for shade prefer rich soil, which is soil high in organic matter. If your soil is not naturally rich, simply add organic matter to improve it. You can use peat moss, leaf mold, dehydrated manure, or compost. The organic matter activates beneficial organisms in the soil and helps it retain moisture and drain better. If a ground cover you would like to grow prefers poor soil, add little or no organic matter when you prepare the soil for planting. Average garden soil has about 25 percent organic matter; rich soil has more than 25 percent, and poor soil has less.

The Importance of pH

The acidity or alkalinity of soil is measured on a pH scale. The pH of the soil is important because it affects a plant's ability to take up nutrients through its roots. A soil's pH is measured on a scale of 1 to 14. A pH of 7 is neutral; a higher rating indicates alkaline soil, a lower rating, acid soil. If you are not sure of the pH of your soil, you can buy a soil test kit at your garden supply store or have a sample tested by your local Cooperative Extension Service or a soil test lab. Soils in the East and the Northwest are generally acid, and soils in the Midwest and Southwest are generally alkaline.

Most ground covers prefer slightly acid to neutral soil, with a pH from 5.5 to 7.0. Some woodland plants like more acid soil, with a pH of 4.5 to 5.5. If a plant needs a soil more acid than yours, you can lower the pH by adding sulfur. Peat moss and many fertilizers also lower pH. If your soil is too acid, you can raise its pH (make it neutral or alkaline) by incorporating limestone. Dolomitic limestone is recommended because it is slow-acting, does not burn plant roots, and contains the essential elements magnesium and calcium.

Fertilizer

A complete fertilizer contains nitrogen, phosphorus, and potassium (potash). The numbers on the label of a package of fertilizer indicate the percentages of each of these elements: 5–10–10, for example, is 5 percent nitrogen, 10 percent phosphate, and 10 percent potash. Most ground covers will benefit if you incorporate a complete fertilizer into the soil while preparing the planting area and follow up with a yearly application each spring when growth starts.

Fertilizer requirements vary from plant to plant; refer to the plant descriptions for specific needs. A fertilizer high in nitrogen (one with a 2:1:1 ratio, for example, such as 10–5–5 or 20–10–10) will promote lush leaf and stem growth and is recommended for foliage plants. A high-nitrogen fertilizer should not, however, be applied to flowering ground covers, because the nitrogen encourages leaf and stem growth at the expense of fruit and flowers. For these ground covers, a 1:2:1 or 1:2:2 ratio, such as 5–10–5 or 5–10–10, is fine.

Phosphorus is necessary for good root growth; unfortunately, it is lacking in many soils. Many gardeners find that incorporating a high-phosphorus fertilizer, such as superphosphate (0–46–0), into the soil several days before planting promotes healthy root growth for many years.

Getting Started

Before you go outside and start to plant your new ground covers, you must do several things to ensure that your investment will have a long and healthy life and will be an asset to your landscape.

Designing with Ground Covers

As we have seen, you can use ground covers for shade in many ways. Keep several things in mind when creating your design. If you are covering a vast expanse, large masses of the same plant often look better than several different plants together. If you choose a flowering ground cover, make sure its color blends with other colors in your garden. When choosing foliage plants, consider leaf size and texture and fall color. You might also consider winter interest; an evergreen will, of course, effectively cover the ground all winter, but a deciduous plant that has brightly colored berries in winter could be equally attractive. Keep plant height in mind; an 18-inch-high ground cover would not make sense planted under low trees and shrubs but might be very effective lining a pathway.

To decide how to lay out the plants in a large area, envision shapes on the ground. You can use stakes and strings or a garden hose to "sketch" out different forms. Ground covers work in formal, geometric beds and borders as well as in informal, flowing curves. The new planting should, however, blend in and harmonize with the rest of your landscape. The height and size of the plants should be in proportion to the overall design. It is very helpful to sketch the design out on graph paper. Using this drawing and the information in each plant description about the growth habits of the different plants, you can determine how many plants you will need to cover a given area.

Buying Ground Covers

Most ground covers are sold in garden centers in containers or flats. Look for plants with healthy, rich green color and dense, compact growth. Select plants that have been well watered and cared for; do not buy plants that have roots growing out the bottom of the pot or that show indications of insects or diseases. Ground cover plants are also sold by many mail-order nurseries. Most nurseries ship plants in spring and fall, in time for planting. If you are ordering plants from a nursery in another part of the country, you may want to specify a shipping date.

Preparing the Soil

Because ground covers live for many years in the same spot, it is worth the effort to prepare the soil very well before planting them. You should not, however, prepare soil that is still wet, because you can ruin it by compacting it. To test whether your soil is ready to be worked, take a handful and squeeze it. If it remains solid and sticky, it is still too wet and cannot be worked. Wait a few days and try again. When it crumbles easily, it is ready. If the soil is dry or dusty, water it well several days before preparing it. If you are making a new bed, first remove all grass, weeds, and soil debris. Add organic matter as needed on top of the soil and mix it in with a spade or Rototiller to a depth of 18 inches. Add a superphosphate fertilizer (0–46–0) at this time, at the rate of 5 pounds per 100 square feet. Adjust the soil pH if necessary. Mix the soil and its amendments thoroughly, rake it level, and allow it to settle for several days before planting. If you're planting between or under existing trees and shrubs, do not dig up the whole area; prepare the soil only where plants will be added so you do not disturb the other roots.

Planting Ground Covers

Your climate will determine when you should plant your ground covers. In very cold climates, planting in spring is recommended because the plants have the long growing season ahead to become established before winter. Ground covers planted in fall in cold areas may not have enough time to establish themselves and may heave out of the ground in winter. In warm places, plant ground covers in early spring, so they are established before summer's heat comes, or in early fall, about two to three months before the first frost.

If you are planting a new bed, lay the plants on the ground in their pots according to the design you sketched out, and move them around until you are satisfied with the arrangement. (Place a board across the bed to walk on so you will not compact the soil.) Space the plants according to how wide they spread, how fast they grow, and how quickly you want to cover the area. The more closely you space plants, the more quickly the area will be covered—but it will also be more expensive, so your budget may also be your guide. As a general rule, space perennials and vines 1 foot apart and shrubs 3 feet apart.

Before planting, water both the new plants and the ground. Dig a hole that is slightly larger than the root ball, and remove the plant from its pot by turning the pot upside down. If necessary, rap the bottom of the pot to loosen the root ball, but never pull a plant out by its stem. Loosen and spread out any roots that are tightly wound around the plant, then set the plant in the hole so it will be growing at the same level as it grew in the pot. Gently firm the soil around the roots.

If the plants are large, refill the hole halfway with soil, fill the hole with water, let it drain, and then fill the hole completely with soil. This will eliminate air pockets and ensure that the roots are in direct contact with soil.

After planting, water the transplants well and continue to water them daily until they show signs of new growth. Building a ring of soil around large plants will create a well that will help draw water to the roots.

Planting on Slopes

If you are planting on a shaded slope, wait for a rainfall so you can check to see if the soil is eroding. If it is, use ground covers with deep roots and plant them in a staggered pattern to best hold the soil in place. Plant the ground covers as you would any others, following the instructions given above. After the plants are in the ground, build the soil up slightly on the downward side of each new plant to help it collect water and become better established.

Caring for Ground Covers

Once your ground covers are planted, you can maintain them easily by performing just a few basic chores each week. The most important aspects of garden care are water and food requirements and weed control.

Watering

Water requirements vary from plant to plant; check the individual plant accounts for specific needs. In general, plants with narrow or needlelike leaves require less water than plants with large leaves. Watering once a week is usually sufficient for a plant that needs average moisture; water more if it is very hot, sunny, or windy.

Fertilizing

Most ground covers benefit from the application of a complete fertilizer in early spring to mid-spring when growth starts. Water the ground well first, apply the fertilizer, and then water again to carry the fertilizer into the root zone. Some gardeners think that plants in shade need extra fertilizer to make up for lack of light. This is not true; plants grown in the shade generally need less fertilizer than plants grown in the sun.

Mulching and Weeding

Mulch is a layer of material, usually organic, that is placed on the ground to act as insulation, keep the soil temperature even, retard evaporation, and suppress weeds. Mulch is especially beneficial to woodland shade plants that grow in rich, moist, cool soil. When ground covers are newly planted, mulch them until they grow into a thick carpet.

There are many different mulches available. When choosing one, consider availability, cost, durability, and appearance. Some good mulches are bark chips, buckwheat hulls, shredded leaves, and pine needles. Peat moss is not a good mulch because it dries out easily. Grass clippings, which must be dried first, are readily available but break down fast.

Remove weeds as soon as they appear. They compete with ground covers for food, water, and light, and they are often breeding grounds for insects and diseases. It is easiest to weed when the ground is wet; weed large areas with a hoe. Pre-emergent herbicides prevent weed seeds from germinating and won't harm ground covers; don't use any other herbicide.

Pruning and Trimming

Ground covers do not need heavy pruning; most need pruning only to keep them neat and attractive. Early spring is the best time to prune woody plants, because the new growth will quickly cover the bare stems. Cut out any dead branches or winter-damaged growing tips, and shape the plants if necessary. You can mow large plantings of some ground covers if they have suffered winter damage; use a rotary mower on its highest setting. Clip back vining ground covers at any time of year if they start to overgrow the area or are growing into or over other plants. Avoid pruning in late summer or fall; it can encourage new growth that may not survive the winter.

Propagation

You can propagate ground covers in a number of ways, depending on the type of plant. Propagating your own plants can greatly cut down the expense of starting a new planting: you can buy just a few plants and, once they have established themselves, increase the planting by division, taking cuttings, or layering.

Division

The easiest way to increase perennial and vining ground covers and some shrubby plants is by division. The best time to divide plants is in early spring when growth starts or in late summer, about two months before the first fall frost. To divide plants, dig them up carefully, taking care to disturb the roots as little as possible. Wash the soil off the roots if you cannot see what you are doing. Pull the plant apart with your hands; some plants have heavy root systems, and you will need to use a spade or trowel. Replant the divisions before the roots dry out. If you divide plants in the late summer, you should prune the tops back by about half to compensate for the lost roots. In spring, prune the tops only if there is a substantial amount of new growth.

Cuttings

Many perennials, vines, and shrubby plants can be propagated from stem cuttings. This method will yield a larger number of plants than division, but it requires more care. The best time to take cuttings from most plants is midsummer to late summer, when growth is neither too soft nor too firm. Choose a shoot that is 3 to 6 inches long and has four to six leaves. Many woody plants root more quickly if there is a piece of the main stem, known as a heel, at the bottom of the cutting.

Remove the bottom two to three leaves and any flowers or flower buds. Place the cutting in a moistened mixture of peat moss and sand. Many woody plants will root more easily and quickly if you dust the nodes with a rooting hormone before you put the cuttings in the medium. The exposed nodes—the scars left when the leaves were removed—must be below the surface of the medium, because it is from the nodes that the new roots will grow. Cover the pot with a clear plastic bag to keep moisture in. Place the container in good light but not direct sun.

Check the cutting for roots in about a month by gently tugging on one of the leaves. If it has not rooted, check it again in another few weeks. Once the cutting has rooted, remove the plastic bag and let the new plant grow (in this pot or in a new pot with potting soil) until it is large enough to transplant to its permanent position.

Layering

You can increase trailing plants and plants with pliable stems by layering. The best time to layer plants is in spring or early summer. Simply secure a trailing stem to the ground with a stick or wire (without breaking it or removing it from the plant) and cover the stem with 1 to 2 inches of soil. Keep the soil moist at all times. You can make a series of layers with long stems by weaving them in and out of the soil. To layer a woody plant, cut into the stem part way on the underside and dust it with rooting hormone before covering it with soil.

Some perennial and vining ground covers may be rooted by fall; woody plants may not root until the following year. As soon as it seems that a large root system has developed, you can cut the stem away from the main plant and transplant it.

Seeds

You can easily grow most perennial ground covers from seeds. Woody plants usually grow more slowly from seeds, and their seeds require a cold period before they germinate, which can make this method of propagation a slow process.

Sow seeds outdoors if they are not too small and if they will grow into fairly large, well-established plants during the first growing season. For herbaceous perennials, plant seeds outdoors from early spring through midsummer. Sow them according to packet directions, in prepared soil, and keep the soil evenly moist until germination occurs.

Start fine seeds, and seeds of plants that take a long time to germinate and grow, indoors in clean, sterile flats or pots using a soilless, pre-moistened growing medium. Put the containers in a clear plastic bag to keep the humidity high, and set them in good light but not direct sun. Once the seeds have germinated, remove the plastic bag and move the container to full sun or under fluorescent lights. Water, preferably from the bottom, to keep the medium evenly moist. When the seedlings have four to six leaves, move them to individual pots to make transplanting easier later on.

Before the new plants can be added to the garden, they must gradually become accustomed to the outdoor environment; this process is called "hardening off." A week before planting time, place the seedlings outdoors in a protected spot during the day and bring them back inside at night. Each day, increase the amount of time they are outside and the amount of light they receive. At the end of the week you can plant them.

Fall and Winter Care

In fall, rake leaves out of the ground covers and do a general garden cleanup. Water the ground deeply—plants will survive the winter better if their roots are not dry. You can spray broadleaf evergreens with antidesiccant to help protect them from sun and wind burn. If your plants are marginally hardy in your zone or if they are in a very windy spot, apply winter protection, such as evergreen boughs, after the ground freezes. Remove it the following spring.

A Note on Plant Names

The common, or English, names of plants are often colorful and evocative: Lady's-Mantle, Japanese Fairy-Bells, and Piggyback Plant. But common names vary widely from region to region—Fringe-Cups and False Alum-Root are both names for the same plant. Sometimes, very different plants may have the same or similar common names; there are two plants called Irish Moss. And some have no common name at all. But every plant, fortunately, is assigned a scientific, or Latin, name that is distinct and unique to that plant. Scientific names are not necessarily more right, but they are standard around the world and governed by an international set of rules. Therefore, even though scientific names may at first seem difficult or intimidating, they are in the long run a simple and sure way of distinguishing one plant from another.

A scientific name has two parts. The first is called the generic name; it tells us to which genus (plural, genera) a plant belongs. The second part of the name tells us the species. (A species is a kind of plant or animal that is capable of reproducing with members of its kind, but genetically isolated from others. *Homo sapiens* is a species.) Most genera have many species; *Cornus,* for example, has about 45. *Cornus canadensis,* Bunchberry, is a species included in this book.

Some scientific names have a third part, which may be in italics or written within single quotation marks in roman type. This third part designates a variety or cultivar; some species may have dozens of varieties or cultivars that differ from the species in plant size, plant form, flower size, or flower color. Technically, a variety is a plant that is naturally produced, while a cultivar (short for "cultivated variety") has been created by a plant breeder. For the purposes of the gardener, they may be treated as the same thing. *Bergenia cordifolia* 'Profusion' is one example.

A hybrid is a plant that is the result of a cross between two genera, two species, or two varieties or cultivars. Sometimes hybrids are given a new scientific name, but they are usually indicated by an × within the scientific name: *Primula × polyantha*, Primrose, is a hybrid in this book.

Organization of the Plant Accounts

The plant accounts in this book are arranged alphabetically by scientific name. If you know only the common name of a ground cover, refer to the index and turn to the page given.

Some accounts in the book deal with a garden plant at the genus level—because the genus includes many similar species that can be treated in more or less the same way in the garden. In these accounts, only the genus name is given at the top of the page; the name of the species, cultivar, or hybrid pictured is given within the text.

One Last Word

You now have all the information you need to begin enhancing your landscape with ground covers for shade. So turn to the descriptions and start choosing the plants that will solve your garden problems and beautify your surroundings.

Ground Covers for Shade

Goutweed *(Aegopodium podagraria)*

When Goutweed, or Bishop's Weed, is not in bloom, it densely covers the ground with a 6-inch-high mat of light green, toothed and divided leaves. In early summer, it sends up 3-inch, flat-topped clusters of white flowers on 12- to 14-inch stems. Goutweed was well named—it grows very fast and can become weedy—but is a useful covering for large areas that you do not want to maintain heavily. 'Variegatum', shown here, has light green leaves edged in white; it is prettier and less aggressive than the species.

GROWING TIPS

Goutweed grows best in partial or full shade. It is not fussy about growing conditions; the soil can be dry or moist but should not be fertilized. The roots spread quickly underground; you can keep them somewhat in check by placing a metal barrier at the edge of the bed. To keep Goutweed from spreading by dropped seeds, remove the flowers as soon as they start to fade. When Goutweed becomes very thick, you can divide or mow it.

Bugleweed *(Ajuga reptans)*

Bugleweed has glossy, oval leaves that form mats of rosettes on the ground. The textured leaves, which are 2–4 inches long, are evergreen or semievergreen in warmer zones. Most Bugleweed varieties have dark green leaves, but there is a variety with bronze leaves, one with purple leaves, and one with variegated leaves in green, white, pink, and purple. Spikes of flowers 3–6 inches high bloom in midspring; they are usually blue to purple, but there is also a variety with white flowers. Bugleweed plants send out runners that form new plants at their ends. Ajuga is very effective planted under trees and shrubs that bloom at the same time in spring.

Growing Tips

Bugleweed prefers partial shade, especially where the climate is hot. It is not fussy about soil as long as it is moist and well drained. Bugleweed plants can easily be divided when they become crowded. You can remove the plants at the ends of the runners to start new plantings.

Lady's-Mantle *(Alchemilla mollis)*

The silvery or gray foliage of Lady's-Mantle forms spreading, mounded clumps and is reason enough to grow the plant. The leaves are round, deeply lobed, and slightly velvety, and are topped by flowers in late spring or early summer. These flowers are yellow-green, have no petals, and appear in feathery sprays 12–15 inches high and 2–3 inches wide. In warmer areas, Lady's-Mantle may be evergreen. It is also sold as *A. vulgaris.*

GROWING TIPS
Plant Lady's-Mantle in partial shade in any garden soil. In hot and dry climates, it benefits from a rich soil that is kept well watered. Dropped seeds self-sow easily, so remove the flowers as they fade if you want to keep the plants from spreading too much. Lady's-Mantle grows best in areas that have freezing temperatures during the winter.

Bog Rosemary *(Andromeda polifolia)* Zone 3

A s the name suggests, Bog Rosemary is a plant that grows in very wet areas and has needlelike leaves like those of the herb Rosemary. The evergreen foliage is gray-green, thick, and slightly fuzzy. In early spring to mid-spring, small, pink, drooping flowers shaped like bells form in dense clusters that completely cover the plant. Bog Rosemary plants grow slowly to 12 inches high and spread slightly.

GROWING TIPS

Bog Rosemary must have rich, very moist, acid soil; it grows best in light to partial shade. Bog Rosemary will not grow well where summer temperatures are high or where freezing temperatures do not occur in winter.

Canada Anemone *(Anemone canadensis)*

The light green leaves at the base of Canada Anemone plants are divided, with 5–7 lobes, and grow at the ends of long leafstalks. Single 2-inch flowers with 5 petal-like sepals appear in early summer on 2-foot stems. They are white with showy yellow stamens and are very attractive. Canada Anemone plants grow quickly and can be invasive; they are best used as a ground cover in large areas.

GROWING TIPS

Plant Canada Anemone in light shade. It grows best in soil that is rich, moist, and well drained. If the plants start to become overcrowded, thin or divide them. Remove flowers before they drop their seeds to prevent Canada Anemone from self-sowing.

Irish Moss *(Arenaria verna)*

Irish Moss forms clumpy, 2-inch-high mats of mosslike foliage. The narrow, ¾-inch leaves are evergreen. Small white flowers, each ½ inch long with 5 round petals, bloom in clusters in late spring or early summer. Irish Moss can tolerate foot traffic and is useful as a ground cover between stepping stones; it can also be used in the rock garden.

GROWING TIPS

Irish Moss prefers partial shade, especially where summers are hot. It will grow in ordinary garden soil but grows best in soil that is slightly acid, moist, and sandy. Divide Irish Moss plants to propagate them.

European Wild Ginger *(Asarum europaeum)*   Zone 5

European Wild Ginger is one of several fast-growing and wide-spreading wild gingers. All have aromatic leaves and rootstocks, scented something like ginger. European Wild Ginger's shiny, leathery, evergreen leaves are heart shaped, 3–6 inches wide, and grow on long leafstalks. Bell-shaped flowers, usually hidden by the foliage, bloom in late spring and summer. They are ½–1 inch across, purplish green on the outside, and deep maroon inside. European Wild Ginger forms a 7-inch-high mat.

GROWING TIPS

European Wild Ginger must have full shade and will grow best in rich, moist soil that is well drained and slightly acid. Because of its growing requirements, it does well in wooded areas and under trees. When European Wild Ginger becomes crowded, divide the creeping rootstocks and reset them 8–12 inches apart. European Wild Ginger will not grow where temperatures do not fall below freezing in winter.

Chinese Astilbe, a dwarf member of the astilbe clan of perennial border plants, has toothed, deeply divided leaves that are somewhat fernlike. Tiny mauve-pink flowers bloom in dense, erect plumes in midsummer to late summer. When in bloom, the plants are 8–12 inches high. The flowers are still attractive after they fade; you can leave them on the plant or use them indoors in dried arrangements. Because of its small size, Chinese Astilbe is a good choice for a rock garden or as a ground cover in front of a shrub border.

Growing Tips

Chinese Astilbe grows best in partial shade in average garden soil. Although it prefers moist soil, it also tolerates drought very well. It is a heavy feeder and benefits from additional fertilizer in midsummer. Divide the plants in spring or fall every 2–3 years. Chinese Astilbe will not grow well in areas that do not have freezing temperatures in winter.

False Rockcress (*Aubrieta deltoidea*) Zone 5

False Rockcress is also called Purple Rockcress because its flowers are typically lavender to purple, although there are also pink varieties. The flowers, which are ¾ inch across, bloom in loose clusters on 3- to 6-inch stems from early to late spring. The evergreen leaves are very crowded along the hairy stems, forming a 2- to 3-inch-high mat.

Growing Tips

Plant False Rockcress in light shade. It will grow best in loose, sandy soil that is moist and well drained. Mulch the soil in summer to keep it cool and moist. After the plants have flowered, clip them back with pruning shears to keep them compact. They may rebloom in fall if they have been clipped. When False Rockcress needs dividing, do it in spring, spacing the new plants 6–8 inches apart. False Rockcress does best in areas where summers are cool and humid.

Bergenia *(Bergenia ciliata)*

Bergenia's fleshy basal leaves form a dense and attractive ground cover. The rounded leaves, which have scalloped, hairy edges, grow to 12 inches long and form 12-inch-high clumps. Showy flowers of white or rose-purple bloom in 9-inch clusters in late spring. Bergenia is a good plant for the shady border or for areas under trees or near ponds.

GROWING TIPS

Plant Bergenia in light shade. It grows in any soil but does best in a soil that is moist, rich, and well drained. Bergenia needs protection from wind, which can tear the leaves. Increase the planting by dividing the clumps in spring. You can also grow Bergenia from seed.

Heartleaf Bergenia *(Bergenia cordifolia)* Zone 3

Heartleaf Bergenia has shiny, medium green, heart-shaped leaves that are 1 foot across and grow in dense clumps at the base of the plant. The fleshy leaves are textured, with crinkled or scalloped edges, and turn red in fall. In late spring, small, single pink flowers appear in nodding clusters on 12- to 18-inch red stems. The variety 'Profusion' is shown here. Siberian Tea, *B. crassifolia,* has smaller leaves with turned-back edges and shorter leafstalks. The leaves of both bergenias may be evergreen in warm areas.

GROWING TIPS
Plant Heartleaf Bergenia in partial shade. It prefers rich, moist, well-drained soil but will tolerate poor, dry growing conditions. The wind can tear the large leaves, so plant it in a protected spot. When the plants become crowded, you can divide them. Heartleaf Bergenia grows best where temperatures are freezing in winter, but it needs winter protection at the coldest limits of its hardiness.

Siberian Bugloss *(Brunnera macrophylla)*

Young Siberian Bugloss plants have small leaves; after several years of growth, the leaves become coarser and much larger, up to 8 inches across. They are dull, dark green, heart shaped, and hairy, growing in a clump at the base of the plant. The leaves of some cultivars are spotted or edged in creamy yellow. In mid-spring, light, airy sprays of small, starlike, bright blue flowers that look like Forget-Me-Nots bloom on 15- to 18-inch stems. This plant is sometimes called *Anchusa myosotidiflora.*

GROWING TIPS

Partial to full shade is a must for Siberian Bugloss. It grows best in moist, cool, acid soil, but it will tolerate many soils, as well as drought. Siberian Bugloss reseeds freely and can become invasive, so cut the flowers off as soon as they fade. Divide the roots when necessary and space the new plants 12 inches apart.

Green-and-Gold *(Chrysogonum virginianum)* Zone 5

As its name suggests, this striking ground cover has bright gold flowers blooming against a background of foliage that is sometimes so dark green it looks almost black. The oval, toothed, hairy leaves cover the 4- to 12-inch-high plants. The flowers, which bloom in spring and summer, have 5 fringed petals and are 1½ inches across. Green-and-Gold makes an especially pretty carpet under trees and shrubs.

GROWING TIPS

Plant Green-and-Gold in partial to full shade. It prefers soil that is rich and well drained, and it grows and flowers best where summers are cool. Apply a summer mulch to keep the soil cool and moist. When Green-and-Gold becomes crowded, divide the plants, spacing the divisions 12 inches apart. In the northern limits of its hardiness, give Green-and-Gold winter protection.

Sweet Fern *(Comptonia peregrina)*

The aromatic leaves of Sweet Fern, or Shrubby Fern, are long, narrow, and notched like those of ferns. This deciduous, shrubby ground cover grows into a dense mass, spreading by underground runners. It can grow as much as 5 feet tall but usually grows much lower. It has small and insignificant green flowers, appearing in catkins. The flowers are followed by small burrlike nuts. Sweet Fern is sometimes sold as *Myrica asplenifolia.*

GROWING TIPS

Sweet Fern is a good cover for a sandy or rocky bank, especially where soil erosion control is needed, because it has a strong root system. It grows equally well in poor, dry soil or rich soil, as long as it is well drained. Plant Sweet Fern in partial shade. It can be propagated by division, by layering, or from seeds.

Lily-of-the-Valley (*Convallaria majalis*)   Zone 4

Well known for its fragrance, Lily-of-the-Valley is also very effective as a ground cover. The foliage, which grows 4–8 inches high from the base of the plant, is upright and pointed. Unfortunately, it can turn brown and become unattractive by midsummer. Bell-shaped, drooping flowers bloom in mid-spring along one side of the 6- to 12-inch flower stalks. Most of the varieties have single, waxy, white flowers, but there are also pink and double-flowered types. Plant Lily-of-the-Valley near walkways so you can enjoy the lovely scent; cut flowers to bring the fragrance indoors.

GROWING TIPS

Plant Lily-of-the-Valley in partial to full shade. It will do best in rich, well-fertilized soil that is moist and well drained. The roots of Lily-of-the-Valley have new growth buds called "pips." When plants become crowded, separate the pips and plant them 4–6 inches apart. Lily-of-the-Valley does not like warm winters.

Bunchberry *(Cornus canadensis)*

Bunchberry, a relative of the dogwood, is a low-growing, woody plant that is a good ground cover under trees or in a woodland garden. It grows only 2–6 inches high but can spread 12 feet across. Its round, dull green leaves are textured, 2 inches long, and pointed; they appear in whorled clusters at the tops of short, upright stems. Bunchberry blooms in late spring. The 1- to 1½-inch flowers are single, with 4–6 white bracts surrounding small greenish flowers. Clusters of red, edible berries form in the fall.

Growing Tips

Bunchberry grows best in partial shade and rich, sandy, acid soil that is moist and well drained. It prefers cool summers and does not like warm winters. The creeping rootstocks can be divided, or new plants can be rooted from stem cuttings.

Japanese Fairy-Bells *(Disporum sessile)*

The narrow, leathery, lance-shaped leaves of Japanese Fairy-Bells are deeply veined along their 4-inch length. The species has green leaves; the leaves of 'Variegatum', shown here, are edged in white. In spring, nodding, bell-shaped flowers appear at the tips of 1- to 2-foot stems. The inch-long blooms are cream to greenish white.

GROWING TIPS

Plant Japanese Fairy-Bells in partial to full shade. They perform best in rich, moist, well-drained soil. Japanese Fairy-Bells are woodland plants; they do well under trees because they do not compete with the tree roots. They spread by creeping underground stems, which can be divided and spaced 2 feet apart when they are crowded, or left undisturbed for many years. Japanese Fairy-Bells do best where they are not subjected to excessive heat.

Longspur Epimedium
(Epimedium grandiflorum)

Zone 5

The flowers of Longspur Epimedium, which are 1–2 inches across, are the largest of any epimedium, blooming in clusters in mid-spring. The spurred flowers may be white, yellow, pink, or violet; 'Rose Queen' is pictured here. Longspur Epimedium is semievergreen and grows 12 inches high. The leaves, which grow in clumps, are heart shaped and finely toothed. New leaves are red in spring and turn bronze in the fall. This species is sometimes sold as *E. macranthum.*

GROWING TIPS

Plant Longspur Epimedium in partial shade. It likes either light or heavy soil that is rich and slightly acid. It prefers moist soil but will tolerate dry conditions as well. Longspur Epimedium very rarely needs dividing, but if necessary, divide when growth starts in spring. Cut the plants back in spring to keep them tidy.

Red Epimedium *(Epimedium × rubrum)*

Red Epimedium is a deciduous plant, growing 12–15 inches high. Bright pink to red flowers with white spurs bloom on wiry stems; the small flowers are sometimes hidden under the foliage. The toothed, heart-shaped leaves grow in clumps. They are light green when they open, often tinged in red, and turn purple in fall before they drop from the plant.

GROWING TIPS

Plant Red Epimedium in partial shade, in either light or heavy soil. It grows best in rich, slightly acid soil that is kept moist, but it will also tolerate dry conditions. If necessary, divide Red Epimedium when growth starts in spring.

Persian Epimedium has green, heart-shaped, finely toothed leaves that are tinged in purple when they open in spring. A robust grower, this epimedium reaches 12 inches tall. Although it is deciduous, it hangs on to its foliage well into fall. Small yellow flowers with red spurs bloom in clusters on wiry stems in mid-spring. 'Sulphureum', shown here, is an excellent variety with yellow and white flowers.

GROWING TIPS

Plant Persian Epimedium in partial shade. It grows in either light or heavy soil, preferably one that is rich, slightly acid, and moist, but it will also tolerate dry conditions. Divide Persian Epimedium if necessary—it very rarely is—when growth starts in spring. Cut the plants back in spring to keep them looking neat.

W inter Creeper is an easy-to-grow evergreen vine that roots as it creeps along the ground. It reaches a height of 1–2 feet and can spread as much as 20 feet across. Its smooth, waxy, oval leaves are up to 2 inches long. Winter Creeper blooms, but the flowers are very small and inconspicuous. Round, pale pink berries that form in the fall open to show red or orange seeds. 'Colorata', Purple Winter Creeper, is slightly lower growing; its leaves turn purple in the fall and winter. 'Silver Queen', Variegated Winter Creeper, seen here, is a taller variety; its leaves are green and creamy white. *E. fortunei* was formerly called *E. radicans.*

GROWING TIPS

Winter Creeper tolerates a wide range of light conditions from full shade to full sun. It does best in acid soil but will grow in any well-drained soil. Winter Creeper is very easy to grow from hardwood cuttings or by layering stems.

Galax *(Galax urceolata)*

Galax is a showy evergreen with clumps of shiny, leathery foliage. The leaves, which grow at the base of the plant, are round to heart shaped, measure 3–4 inches across, and turn bronze in the fall. Galax plants grow 6–10 inches high and an equal distance across. Tiny white flowers bloom in late spring and early summer. They grow in slender spikes at the tops of 2½-foot, leafless stems. Galax combines well with ferns and other shade-loving plants in the woodland garden. It is sometimes sold as *G. aphylla*.

GROWING TIPS

Galax likes partial to full shade and rich, acid soil. Mulch the soil in early spring to keep it cool and moist during the summer. Galax grows best where summers are not too hot and winters are freezing. Divide Galax in spring or fall when needed, or root pieces of the rhizomatous root to propagate new plants.

Sweet Woodruff (*Galium odoratum*)

Sweet Woodruff has creeping, somewhat weak stems that are encircled by whorls of lance-shaped, 1-inch, shiny green leaves. The plants grow 6–12 inches high and spread to 2 feet across. In spring, small, white, star-shaped flowers bloom in clusters. The aromatic leaves and stems of Sweet Woodruff are used to flavor May wine. This plant was formerly known as *Asperula odorata*.

GROWING TIPS

Sweet Woodruff likes a spot in partial to full shade where soil is slightly acid, rich, moist, and well drained. If the soil is too poor or too dry, the leaves will turn brown and the plants will be stunted. Cut Sweet Woodruff back each spring, or it will become leggy. If the center starts to die out, divide it in spring. Sweet Woodruff benefits from winter protection in the northern limits of its hardiness.

Wintergreen *(Gaultheria procumbens)*

Wintergreen, or Teaberry, is a shrubby, evergreen ground cover. Small, drooping, bell-shaped white flowers bloom in spring or early summer, followed in fall by attractive red berries. The berries are edible and have a wintergreen aroma and flavor. Wintergreen plants grow 3–5 inches high and spread to 12–18 inches across. The bristly, oval leaves are 2 inches long and shiny green, turning red or purple in cold winters. Use Wintergreen under trees or in places where it can cascade over and around rocks or a wall.

GROWING TIPS

Wintergreen likes partial shade. It will grow only in acid soil, preferably one that is rich, moist, and well drained. In hot areas, keep it heavily mulched so it will grow to its full potential. Wintergreen is easy to propagate from cuttings, by division, or by layering.

Box Huckleberry *(Gaylussacia brachycera)*   Zone 5

Box Huckleberry is a slow-growing evergreen that spreads by underground stems. It has upright branches growing 6–16 inches high and bright green, shiny, oval leaves that are 1–1½ inches long. Tiny, bell-shaped, white or pink flowers bloom in spikes in spring and summer. These are followed by edible—but not very tasty—blue berries in fall. Box Huckleberry is a good plant to use in rock gardens or to cover the ground in small spaces.

GROWING TIPS

Plant Box Huckleberry in a spot with partial to full shade. It grows best in moist, rich, acid soil. Anytime you want to increase the planting, dig and divide the creeping roots.

Johnson's Blue Cranesbill

(*Geranium* 'Johnson's Blue')

Zone 4

A hybrid of the perennial geranium, Johnson's Blue Cranesbill is one of the truest blue flowers you can find for a ground cover. The plants grow to 2 feet high and spread to 2–3 feet across. Johnson's Blue Cranesbill has a long and profuse flowering season, beginning in early summer. The flowers are single and 1½–2 inches across. They are medium blue with darker blue veins, making a pleasing contrast to the lobed and dissected foliage.

GROWING TIPS

Johnson's Blue Cranesbill prefers partial shade, and it grows best in rich, well-drained soil. In hot climates, it must be grown in shade and evenly moist soil. When Johnson's Blue becomes crowded, divide it in spring or fall.

Blood-red Cranesbill *(Geranium sanguineum)*

Don't confuse this plant with the annual garden geranium; they are of different genera and very different in appearance. Blood-red Cranesbill is a mounded or trailing perennial, growing 9–18 inches tall and spreading to 24 inches across. The round, hairy leaves, which are lobed or heavily dissected, are medium to dark green and turn red in the fall. Flowers, which have 5 rounded petals, bloom from late spring through summer. The flowers are typically light pink to reddish purple, but there is also a white variety. The variety *striatum*, seen here, has pink flowers with crimson veins. It is low-growing, reaching only 10 inches in height.

GROWING TIPS

Blood-red Cranesbill grows best in light to partial shade. It prefers soil that is rich, moist, and well drained, but it will tolerate dry soil as well. Blood-red Cranesbill can be sheared back if it becomes lanky, but this trimming is rarely necessary. Divide the clumps in spring or fall if they become crowded.

Ivy (*Hedera*)

Ivies are evergreen vines that are among the most popular ground covers for both flat areas and slopes. When they are allowed to creep along the ground, they have lobed leaves and they rarely flower. Once ground cover ivies grow upright, the leaves change shape and lose their lobes, and the plants flower. Algerian Ivy, *H. canariensis,* has 5- to 8-inch mature leaves and forms a mat 12 inches high. It is hardy to zone 8. English Ivy, *H. helix,* pictured, has 2- to 5-inch leaves and forms a 6-inch-high mat. It is hardy to zone 6.

GROWING TIPS

Ivy grows best in partial to full shade. It prefers rich, moist, well-drained soil but tolerates poor, dry soil. Prune ivy as often as necessary to control and direct its growth, especially around low-growing shrubs. Ivy will grow up wherever it finds a suitable surface, so keep an eye on it if you don't want this to happen.

Siebold Plantain-lily *(Hosta sieboldiana)*

With its blue, heart-shaped, deeply quilted leaves, Siebold, or Blue-leaved, Plantain-lily is striking as an accent plant or a ground cover for a large area. The leaves grow to 15 inches across. Lavender, 1½-inch flowers, often hidden by the leaves, bloom on short stalks in early summer to midsummer. 'Elegans', seen here, has larger, 18-inch leaves. 'Frances Williams' grows 3 feet tall and has blue leaves edged in golden yellow. Siebold Plantain-lily is sometimes sold as *H. glauca*.

GROWING TIPS

Like all hostas, Siebold Plantain-lily is very easy to grow and can be used singly or massed. It grows best in partial shade and rich, moist, well-drained soil. Hosta leaves do not appear until mid-spring; you can fill in the space before they open with early-flowering spring bulbs for an attractive effect. Once the leaves have opened fully, be on the lookout for snails and slugs hiding underneath. Divide Siebold Plantain-lily anytime it becomes crowded.

Houttuynia *(Houttuynia cordata)*

Houttuynia has dark green foliage tinged with metallic red that turns purple in fall. Spreading by underground stems, it grows 18 inches across and 12 inches high. Its citrus-scented leaves are heart shaped and 2–3 inches long. Houttuynia blooms in summer; the flowers are white and cone shaped in the center, surrounded by a rim of bracts. 'Cameleon', the variety pictured, grows 6–9 inches high and has variegated leaves of yellow, green, bronze, and red.

GROWING TIPS

Houttuynia prefers partial to full shade. It requires very moist, rich soil and will even grow in water or along the edges of streams or ponds. Divide Houttuynia in spring or fall if necessary.

Crested Iris (*Iris cristata*)

A miniature version of the Bearded Iris, Crested Iris too has 3 erect petals called standards and 3 drooping petals called falls. The faintly fragrant flowers bloom in mid-spring. They may be lavender, light blue, or white; the petals have hairy yellow markings called crests. Crested Irises grow 4–6 inches high and form dense, spreading mats with sword-shaped, light green foliage. They are attractive in rock gardens, along steps, near the waterside, or in front of larger perennials or shrubs.

GROWING TIPS

Crested Iris prefers partial shade and rich, acid, evenly moist soil. It grows best in areas that have freezing temperatures in winter. Propagate Crested Irises when they become crowded by dividing them.

Yellow Archangel (*Lamiastrum galeobdolon*)

Yellow Archangel has square, hairy stems and dark green, toothed leaves that emit a sharp odor when rubbed. The yellow flowers, which sometimes have brown spots and are lipped like small snapdragons, bloom in whorls in late spring and early summer. The plants grow 8–12 inches high and spread rapidly to 2 feet or more across, rooting as they grow. The leaves are heart shaped and 1½–3 inches long. 'Herman's Pride', seen here, has silvery leaves veined in green. Yellow Archangel is evergreen where winter temperatures do not drop below 10° F. It is sometimes sold as *Lamium galeobdolon* or *Galeobdolon luteum*.

GROWING TIPS

Yellow Archangel likes partial to full shade and therefore grows well in a woodland garden. It tolerates any garden soil but grows best in soil that is rich and moist. Once established, it is fairly drought tolerant. Yellow Archangel can become invasive; keep it in check with an underground barrier. To propagate, divide it or take stem cuttings.

Spotted Dead Nettle *(Lamium maculatum)*

Spotted Dead Nettle is similar to Yellow Archangel, except its flowers are purple, pink, or white, and its growth is not as invasive. The plants grow 8–12 inches high and spread to 2 feet across. The heart-shaped leaves are toothed, 1½–2 inches long, and dark green with a white stripe along the central vein. They may turn pink or purple in the fall. The cultivar 'Variegatum' has a silver stripe on the leaves; 'White Nancy', pictured, has silver leaves with green margins. Use Spotted Dead Nettle in rock gardens or under trees and shrubs.

GROWING TIPS

Plant Spotted Dead Nettle in partial to full shade. It grows best in rich, moist soil but will tolerate poor soil and dry conditions once established. It can be propagated by stem cuttings, root division, or from seeds.

Coast Leucothoe *(Leucothoe axillaris)*

An evergreen shrub, Coast Leucothoe has arching branches covered with leathery, shiny foliage that turns red or bronze in the winter. The leaves are pointed and oval to lance shaped. Urn-shaped white flowers are borne in spring on 1- to 2-inch clusters that appear in the leaf axils. Coast Leucothoe may grow as tall as 5 feet but is more vigorous if kept to 2 feet.

GROWING TIPS

Coast Leucothoe prefers light shade and needs protection from winter sun and wind or the leaves will burn. It likes an extra-rich, moist, well-drained soil. Propagate Coast Leucothoe by dividing the underground runners or from stem cuttings or seeds. Cut the oldest branches to the ground occasionally to keep the plant compact.

Creeping Lily-Turf *(Liriope spicata)* Zone 5

Creeping Lily-Turf has tufts of grassy, narrow leaves that are usually dark green, although one variety has striped leaves. The plants grow 8–10 inches high and spread to 18 inches across. The flowers, which may be white, lilac, or blue, appear in 4- to 8-inch spikes in late summer and fall and are often partially hidden by the foliage. Creeping Lily-Turf can be used on slopes, large flat areas, under trees and shrubs, or by the seashore. It may be evergreen where winter temperatures do not drop below freezing.

GROWING TIPS

Creeping Lily-Turf grows in a wide range of light conditions from full shade to full sun. It tolerates poor, dry soil but grows better in fertile, sandy soil that is moist and well drained. If the foliage becomes brown over the winter, mow the planting in early spring before growth starts. Divide Creeping Lily-Turf when necessary.

Moneywort *(Lysimachia nummularia)*

Moneywort got one of its common names because the shiny, round, ¾-inch leaves look like coins. It got its other name, Creeping Jennie, because of its trailing habit. The leaves appear along stems that grow only 1–2 inches tall but creep and root rapidly to form plants 2–3 feet across. Inch-long, cup-shaped yellow flowers bloom in the leaf axils in spring and summer. Because it grows rapidly, Moneywort does best in large areas. It can also be used near water. The slower growing cultivar 'Aurea', seen here, has yellow leaves.

GROWING TIPS
Moneywort tolerates a wide range of light conditions, from full shade in hot areas to full sun in cool climates. It likes a rich, moist soil. Moneywort can be very invasive and may need frequent pruning and dividing if grown in a small area. Divide in spring or fall when necessary.

Creeping Mahonia *(Mahonia repens)*

Zone 6

Creeping Mahonia is an evergreen shrub with stiff, leathery, compound leaves. Each leaf has 3–7 spiny, blue-green leaflets that turn bronze or purple in winter. Fragrant yellow flowers bloom in clusters at the ends of the branches in the spring. In fall, edible dark blue berries that resemble grapes appear. The plants grow 1 foot tall and spread by underground stems to 6 feet across.

GROWING TIPS

Creeping Mahonia likes partial to full shade and rich, acid soil that is moist and well drained. Propagate Creeping Mahonia by rooting stem cuttings or by dividing the underground stems.

Mazus *(Mazus reptans)*

A mat-forming ground cover, Mazus grows only 2 inches high and spreads to 18 inches across, rooting as it creeps. It has bright green, inch-long leaves that are toothed and lance shaped. The flowers, which are white, blue, or purple with yellow centers spotted in purple, bloom in 1-sided clusters at the ends of the branches in spring and summer. Mazus is evergreen where winter temperatures do not drop below 20° F. It withstands foot traffic and can be used between stepping stones.

GROWING TIPS

Mazus will grow equally well in partial shade or sun. It prefers moist, well-drained soil and can become invasive if the soil is too rich. When Mazus becomes crowded, it can be divided.

Partridge-Berry (*Mitchella repens*)

A woody evergreen, Partridge-Berry has small, round, dark green leaves with white veins. Fragrant, funnel-shaped, ½-inch-long flowers bloom in pairs at the ends of short stems that grow from the leaf axils. The flowers, which may be pink or white, are followed by ¼-inch red berries. Often the flowers and the berries are present at the same time. Partridge-Berry plants grow 1–2 inches high and spread by slender rooting stems to 1–2 feet across.

GROWING TIPS

Partridge-Berry prefers partial to full shade and the rich, moist, acid soil of a woodland garden. It is often slow to establish itself, but once it has, it will grow quickly. Propagate Partridge-Berry by division or from stem or root cuttings. Partridge-Berry needs freezing temperatures in winter.

Forget-Me-Not *(Myosotis scorpioides)*

Perennial Forget-Me-Not grows 6–8 inches high and spreads 15 inches wide on creeping roots. The leaves are narrow and oblong; the small, tubular, 5-lobed flowers are blue with a pink, yellow, or white eye. Blooms appear in delicate, airy clusters at the ends of the stems in spring and early summer. The variety *semperflorens,* seen here, has a longer blooming period. Forget-Me-Not looks best when combined with spring-flowering bulbs and other perennials. This plant is sometimes listed as *M. palustris.*

Growing Tips

Grow Forget-Me-Not in partial to full shade in rich, moist soil. Individual plants may not be long-lived, but Forget-Me-Not self-sows and new plants start easily. Forget-Me-Not does best in cool climates. Increase plants by division or from seeds.

Blue-Eyed Mary *(Omphalodes verna)*

Blue-Eyed Mary grows 8 inches tall and spreads by fast-growing stems to 2 feet across. The stems root as they creep along the ground. The leaves are lance to heart shaped, larger at the base of the plant than they are along the stems. The flowers resemble those of the Forget-Me-Not, which is why Blue-Eyed Mary is sometimes called Creeping Forget-Me-Not. The ½-inch, tubular, 5-lobed blooms are blue with a white center. They appear in spring in loose clusters.

GROWING TIPS

Blue-Eyed Mary grows best in partial shade. The soil should be cool and may be either moist or dry. In hot areas, a mulch will help to extend the life of the plant and the blooming period. When Blue-Eyed Mary plants become crowded, divide them in spring or fall.

Black Mondo Grass
(Ophiopogon planiscapus 'Arabicus') Zone 7

B lack Mondo Grass has tufts of thick, grasslike, evergreen leaves. The leaves are arching and grow from the base of the plant. They are green when new, changing to purplish black as they mature. The plants grow 8–10 inches high and 1 foot across. Nodding, ¼-inch flowers bloom in loose, erect clusters in summer. The blooms, which are often partially hidden by the leaves, are white, pink, or purple and are followed by blue berries. Black Mondo Grass can be used as an edging, under trees and shrubs, or at the seashore.

GROWING TIPS
Black Mondo Grass grows best in partial to full shade. It will grow in any garden soil and tolerates heat and drought as long as it is in the shade. Divide Black Mondo Grass when it becomes crowded. Cut the foliage back in early spring before new growth starts if the leaves become unattractive during winter.

Alleghany Spurge *(Pachysandra procumbens)*   Zone 5

The stems of Alleghany Spurge are trailing at first but they later form erect clumps 8–10 inches high. Mature plants have a spread of 15 inches. The oval, whorled leaves are 3 inches long and dull green mottled in gray. The flowers are greenish white to purple and bloom in spikes in early spring to mid-spring but they are not showy. Alleghany Spurge is deciduous through zone 7 and evergreen in zone 8.

GROWING TIPS

Alleghany Spurge must have partial to full shade; when it receives too much light, the leaves turn yellow. It grows best in rich, cool, moist soil that is neutral to acid, and once established, it tolerates drought. Protect the plants from winter sun and wind to prevent leaf burn. Alleghany Spurge will not grow well· in zones 9–10.

Pachysandra *(Pachysandra terminalis)*

An evergreen ground cover, Pachysandra, or Japanese Spurge, grows 6–12 inches high and spreads to 3 feet across by underground runners. The thick, glossy leaves have toothed edges and are dark green and up to 2–4 inches long. White flowers bloom in rounded spikes in mid-spring, but Pachysandra is better known for its foliage. The cultivar 'Silver Edge' has leaves with narrow, white margins.

GROWING TIPS

Grow Pachysandra in partial to full shade; too much light will turn the leaves yellow. It grows in any moist, ordinary soil but grows best in soil that is rich and neutral to acid. Pachysandra must have freezing temperatures during the winter. The plants may be slow to start but will form a dense cover once established. Large plantings can be pruned back and edged as needed. Propagate Pachysandra by division or from stem cuttings.

Oregon Boxwood *(Paxistima myrsinites)*

If you need a neat, compact, fine-textured, shrubby ground cover, Oregon Boxwood is a good choice. The small, shiny, dark green leaves appear on stiff branches and are evergreen. The flowers, which bloom in early summer, are either greenish white or reddish but are inconspicuous. Oregon Boxwood grows 1½–2 feet tall and spreads to 6 feet across.

GROWING TIPS

Plant Oregon Boxwood in partial shade. It grows best in rich, slightly acid soil that is moist and well drained, but will tolerate poor soil. Oregon Boxwood grows best in areas where humidity is high and temperatures go below 30° F in winter. Propagate new plants by division or from cuttings.

74 GROUND COVERS FOR SHADE

Creeping Phlox *(Phlox stolonifera)*

Creeping Phlox grows 10–12 inches high and 18 inches across. The stems grow quickly and root easily as they spread along the ground. The leaves are ¾ inch long and oval. The flowers, which bloom in mid-spring, are white, pink, rose, lavender, purple, or blue; the variety 'Blue Ridge' is pictured. Wild Sweet William, *P. divaricata,* is another low-growing phlox that thrives in shade. It typically has lavender-blue flowers, but there is a white-flowering variety.

GROWING TIPS

Most phlox species grow in full sun, but Creeping Phlox likes partial shade, and Wild Sweet William likes partial to full shade. Both grow best in soil that is rich, moist, and slightly acid. After the plants have bloomed, shear them back to ensure compact growth. Make sure air circulation is good to avoid mildew problems. Divide phlox as necessary or take stem cuttings to grow new plants.

Creeping Polemonium *(Polemonium reptans)*   Zone 4

Growing 8–12 inches high, Creeping Polemonium is more correctly a spreading, not a creeping, plant. Its narrow, lance-shaped leaflets are arranged ladder-like on the stem, which is why this plant is sometimes called Creeping Jacob's Ladder. Light blue, ½-inch-wide flowers bloom in loose, nodding clusters in late spring and early summer. Use Creeping Polemonium in shady rock gardens or under trees and shrubs.

GROWING TIPS
Creeping Polemonium is easy to grow in partial shade. It likes a moist, extra-rich, well-drained soil. Leaf tips may brown during the summer unless the soil is kept very moist. You can increase Creeping Polemonium by dividing it in spring. It self-sows easily; to prevent it from becoming invasive, remove the flowers before they set seed.

Primrose *(Primula × polyantha)*

These hybrid primroses have clumps of oblong, textured leaves at their bases. The flowers, which are 1–1½ inches across, bloom in early spring in tight, rounded clusters in shades of white, yellow, gold, orange, red, pink, blue, or purple. Each flower has a yellow center. The flowering stems reach 12 inches high. 'Pacific Giant' is a group of hybrids with 2-inch flowers. Use primroses in the shaded rock garden, in a border, or under trees and shrubs.

GROWING TIPS

This is the easiest primrose to grow, but it can be short-lived, especially if the plants are not divided frequently. Grow primroses from seeds sown in spring. Plant them in partial shade; they will do best in moist, fertile soil that is well drained and slightly acid. They prefer a climate where humidity is high. Mulch primroses in hot climates to keep the soil cool and moist.

English Primrose *(Primula vulgaris)*

Zone 5

English Primrose has basal, wrinkled, lance-shaped leaves with crinkled margins. The plants grow to 6 inches high. Flowers bloom in spring on slightly hairy stalks. English Primrose blooms are white, yellow, pale orange, red, pink, lavender, blue, and purple. The Barnhaven hybrids are vigorous, hardier plants with pastel flowers. English Primroses are often sold as *P. acaulis*.

GROWING TIPS

Plant English Primrose in rich, moist soil in light shade. It needs good drainage and protection from sun. Divide the plants every 3–4 years to improve vigor and increase flowering. English Primrose is easily propagated from seed.

Self Heal *(Prunella grandiflora)*

Some members of the genus *Prunella* can be garden weeds, but this one, Self Heal, is used as an ornamental planting in rock gardens or shaded wildflower gardens. The plants grow 12 inches high, with flowering stems growing above mats of toothed leaves that have prominent veins on the undersides. Dense clusters or spikes of flowers bloom in summer; they close and point upward when the weather is dry but open when it is moist. The flowers are mostly bluish purple, but some kinds, including 'Rosea', seen here, have pink or rose flowers.

GROWING TIPS

In warm climates, grow Self Heal in partial shade and moist, rich soil. Where it is cooler, it tolerates sun and ordinary garden soil. Self Heal is easy to propagate by division or from seeds in early spring.

Mountain Lungwort *(Pulmonaria montana)* Zone 4

The coarse, hairy, broadly oval basal leaves of Mountain Lungwort grow in clumps 15 inches high and 12–18 inches wide. Flowering stems emerge before the leaves in mid-spring. The funnel-shaped, violet flowers bloom in nodding clusters. The variety 'Salmon Glow', seen here, has deep coral-red flowers that attract hummingbirds. Mountain Lungwort is a good plant for shady walkways and woodland gardens. It is often listed as *P. rubra*.

GROWING TIPS

Mountain Lungwort grows in partial or full shade and moist garden soil with average fertility. The plants may wilt if the soil becomes dry but they will quickly revive when watered. Mountain Lungwort grows by creeping roots that may be divided in fall or early spring to start new plants. You can also propagate new plants from seeds. Mountain Lungwort will be at its best if soil is kept cool and moist during the summer with the aid of a mulch. It needs freezing temperatures in the winter.

Bethlehem Sage *(Pulmonaria saccharata)*

The coarse, pointed basal leaves of Bethlehem Sage are dark green with white spots. They form clumps 8–14 inches high and 12–24 inches wide. Tubular flowers, which are either white or reddish purple, bloom in nodding terminal clusters in mid-spring. The flowering stems appear before the leaves, but the leaves are fully developed by the time the plant is in full bloom. 'Mrs. Moon', pictured here, is a common variety with pink buds that open into blue flowers. Bethlehem Sage does well along shaded paths and in woodland gardens.

GROWING TIPS

Bethlehem Sage prefers full shade and moist garden soil with average fertility. The plants grow by creeping roots, which may be divided in fall or early spring. Plants may also be propagated from seeds. Bethlehem Sage does not grow well where winter temperatures are mild, and does best when the soil is kept cool and moist during the summer with the aid of a mulch.

Indicum Dwarf Azalea *(Rhododendron indicum)* Zone 6

These evergreen azalea hybrids are valued for their late-spring and early-summer bloom. Although we usually think of azaleas as shrubs, these hybrids include some dwarf varieties that grow 6–18 inches high and spread to 30 inches across; they are quite useful as ground covers. 'Balsaminiflorum', pictured here, has double, salmon-pink flowers. 'Flame Creeper' has orange-red flowers. 'Kozan', which has delicate, shell-pink flowers, is the lowest growing of the three.

GROWING TIPS

Indicum Dwarf Azaleas grow best in partial shade in rich, light soil that is acid and very well drained. Water them often so the soil is always evenly moist. Like all azaleas, Indicum Dwarf Azaleas can be propagated from cuttings or seeds. All azaleas form their flower buds in the fall for bloom the following spring, so prune them immediately after flowering to ensure formation of new shoots with flower buds.

Kurume Azalea *(Rhododendron kiusianum)*

These compact, dense, evergreen azaleas are profuse bloomers. They have small, dark leaves and small, single or double flowers, which appear in mid-spring. Kurume Azaleas reach 3 feet in height. Among the most popular varieties are 'Coral Bells', with double pink blooms; 'Hino-crimson' (shown here), bright red; 'Hinodegiri', cerise red; and 'Snow' and 'Album', both white.

GROWING TIPS

Kurume Azaleas grow best in partial shade and, like all azaleas, should be kept out of afternoon sun. They do best in rich, acid soil that is light and well drained. Water them often to keep the soil evenly moist. All azaleas have shallow roots; they benefit from a mulch to keep them cool and moist. Be very careful not to disturb or damage the roots when weeding around any azalea plant. If the leaves of any azalea turn yellow, check the pH of the soil; apply iron chelate to increase acidity.

North Tisbury Azalea
(*Rhododendron* North Tisbury)

Zone 6

These hybrids were mostly derived from *R. rakaharai,* a small-leaved, low-growing, evergreen azalea. The branches of North Tisbury Azaleas spread to 4 feet wide, and the plants will grow to 15 inches high. 'Alexander' has bright salmon-red flowers in early summer and fine-textured foliage that turns bronze in winter. 'Joseph Hill' has rich red flowers in early summer. 'Pink Pancake', shown here, has pink, ruffled flowers in early summer and is low-growing. 'Late Love' has rosy-pink flowers in early summer to midsummer.

GROWING TIPS
North Tisbury Azaleas grow best in partial shade and rich, acid soil that is light and well drained. Water them often so the soil is evenly moist. Like all azaleas, they should be planted where they are protected from drying winds and winter sun, and they will not grow or flower well where freezing temperatures do not occur in winter.

Robin Hill Azalea *(Rhododendron Robin Hill)* Zone 6

These evergreen azaleas have large, beautiful flowers in predominantly soft pastel colors. They bloom in mid-spring to late spring. Robin Hill Azaleas grow 12–15 inches high and spread to 18–30 inches across. The branches are covered with 2½-inch leaves. 'Betty Ann Voss' has pale pink, double, hose-in-hose flowers (that is, one flower appears to grow inside another). 'Mrs. Hagar' has double, vibrant pink flowers that look like miniature camellias. 'Hilda Niblett', pictured, has soft pink flowers with deep rose markings. 'Sir Rob-

ert', which has large ruffled flowers ranging from white to pale salmon-pink, grows larger than the others, to 2 feet high.

GROWING TIPS

Like all azaleas, Robin Hill hybrids grow best in partial shade and rich, light, acid, well-drained soil that is kept evenly moist. See Indicum, Kurume, and North Tisbury azaleas for additional growing information.

Irish Moss *(Sagina subulata)*

Irish Moss forms an evergreen mat or spongy mound that grows 1–4 inches high and spreads to 12 inches or more across. As the common name suggests, the ¼-inch-long leaves are mosslike. White flowers bloom atop the plant during the summer. The cultivar 'Aurea', pictured, which is called Scotch Moss, has golden-green leaves. As Irish Moss tolerates foot traffic, it can be used successfully between stepping stones; it also works well in rock gardens. It is sometimes confused with *Arenaria verna,* a very different plant with the same common name.

GROWING TIPS

Irish Moss grows best in partial shade; you can use it as a substitute for true mosses, which need deep shade. It prefers moist, fertile soil but it tolerates dry, sandy soil as well. Be sure to take precautions against snails and slugs, which can be pests. Propagate Irish Moss by division or from seeds in the spring.

Sweet Box (*Sarcococca hookerana humilis*) Zone 6

Sometimes called Dwarf Himalayan Sweet Box, this evergreen shrub grows 6–24 inches high and spreads slowly to 8 feet across by sending up new branches from underground. The narrow, thin leaves are 2–3½ inches long, leathery, and shiny dark green. Small, fragrant white flowers bloom in racemes among the leaves in late winter and spring. Small black or red berries form in fall and last through winter. Sweet Box makes a good ground cover under trees.

GROWING TIPS

Sweet Box likes a spot in light to full shade; it will produce more flowers and berries in light shade. It prefers fertile, acid soil that is moist and well drained. Be careful to protect it from winter sun or the leaves will burn. Increase Sweet Box by rooting stem cuttings, by dividing the underground branches, or from seeds.

Strawberry Geranium *(Saxifraga stolonifera)*   Zone 7

Sometimes known as Mother-of-Thousands, Strawberry Geranium spreads quickly by producing many runners that form small plantlets at their ends. An evergreen, it has round, hairy, 4-inch leaves with scalloped edges. The leaves are dark green with white veins on the top and red on the undersides. They grow in rosettes 5 inches high; a clump with its runners can spread to 18 or more inches across. Inch-long white flowers bloom in loose clusters on 6- to 12-inch stems in early summer. This plant is sometimes sold as *S. sarmentosa*.

GROWING TIPS

Strawberry Geranium grows in partial shade, looking its best when it receives morning sun and afternoon shade. It needs sandy, slightly acid to alkaline soil that is well drained and evenly moist. Strawberry Geranium plants can be divided, but the easiest way to propagate them is by removing and rooting the plantlets that grow at the ends of the runners.

London Pride *(Saxifraga × urbium)*

London Pride's toothed, round or oval leaves form carpets of shiny, evergreen rosettes. The 2½-inch leaves, which have red undersides, change from yellow-green when young to dark green when mature. The rosettes grow to 6 inches high and spread slowly to 12 inches across. Pink ¼-inch flowers bloom in clusters 8–10 inches above the foliage in early summer. Use London Pride in a rock garden, under trees and shrubs, or as a border plant. It is sometimes sold as *S. umbrosa*.

GROWING TIPS

The ideal growing conditions for London Pride are partial shade, protection from afternoon sun, and sandy, alkaline to slightly acid soil that is moist and well drained. It does not grow well where summers are hot and dry. When the rosettes become crowded, they should be divided. New plants can also be grown from seeds.

Two-row Stonecrop *(Sedum spurium)*   Zone 3

Two-row Stonecrop will spread quickly by trailing stems to form a mat 3–6 inches high and 1–2 feet across. The oval, 1-inch leaves are toothed. In spring, summer, and fall, the foliage is dark green; it turns red in winter before it begins to fall from the plants. Half-inch white to pink flowers bloom in flat clusters in midsummer to late summer on 9-inch stems. 'Dragon's Blood', pictured, has deep rose to red flowers; its mature foliage is tinged bronzy-purple on the margins. 'Splendens' has large, deep carmine flowers.

GROWING TIPS

Two-row Stonecrop grows well in light to partial shade. Because it is a succulent plant, it prefers a sandy, poor, dry soil with excellent drainage—especially during the winter. Although it spreads quickly, it is easy to control because it is shallow rooted. New plants are easy to propagate from leaf and stem cuttings or by division. Two-row Stonecrop is sometimes called *S. stoloniferum*.

Reeves Skimmia *(Skimmia reevesiana)*

Reeves Skimmia is a dense, mounded, evergreen shrub, growing 18–24 inches high and wide. The dull green foliage measures 3–5 inches long. Separate male and female flowers—both white—bloom on each plant in clusters in early spring to mid-spring. The male flowers are fragrant. The female flowers form round ½-inch berries in the fall, which are yellow at first, changing to dull red when ripe. The berries last well through winter and into the following spring. Reeves Skimmia is often used in rock gardens or planted under trees and shrubs. It tolerates seashore conditions and also does well in the city because it is very resistant to air pollution.

Growing Tips

Reeves Skimmia needs partial to full shade, and it prefers moist, rich, acid, well-drained soil. It is a low-maintenance plant and rarely requires any other care except protection from winter sun to avoid leaf burn. The plants can be increased from cuttings or seeds.

Comfrey *(Symphytum grandiflorum)*

Comfrey is a rapid-growing ground cover, reaching 8 inches in height and 2 feet in width. Its hairy stems spread by rooting at their tips. Large, oval, hairy leaves grow from the base of the plant. In milder climates, Comfrey plants may hold on to their leaves during the winter. Bell-shaped, white to pale yellow flowers with 5 lobes bloom above the dark green foliage in nodding clusters on 12-inch stems. Comfrey is often sold as *Pulmonaria lutea;* it resembles *P. montana* (Mountain Lungwort), except its flowers are yellow.

GROWING TIPS

One of the best plants for dry shade, Comfrey prefers partial to full shade and dry, well-drained soil; it is very tolerant of poor growing conditions. Increase plantings by division or from seeds.

Spreading English Yew
(Taxus baccata 'Repandens')

An evergreen conifer, Spreading English Yew has glossy, slightly curved, 1- to 1¼-inch needles that have 2 pale green lines on the undersides. The needles are usually arranged in a flat plane on the branches. The plants typically grow 2 feet high and 6 feet wide, although very old plants may be larger. The branches spread horizontally, dipping slightly at the tips, and give the plants a flat-topped or sweeping appearance. The red to olive-brown berries form only on female plants. The berries, needles, and bark of all yews are toxic.

GROWING TIPS
Spreading English Yew grows well in partial shade. Soil should be fertile, neutral to slightly acid, moist, and well drained. In the winter, the soil must have excellent drainage, and the plants should be protected from sun and wind. Spreading English Yew will not grow in hot, dry climates. The bark is tender and should be protected from damage by lawn mowers.

Fringe-Cups *(Tellima grandiflora)*

Also known as False Alum-Root, Fringe-Cups has hairy, round to heart-shaped, 4-inch leaves that form a 12-inch-high clump at the base of the plant. The leaves are pink when they first appear in spring, later turn bright green, and become red in fall. The nodding, bell-shaped flowers are green when they first open in late spring and change to pink or red. They bloom on 2-foot stems and have fringed petals. The cultivar 'Rubra' has attractive maroon foliage. Fringe-Cups spreads by creeping roots. It is evergreen in milder climates.

GROWING TIPS

Fringe-Cups prefers light shade and cool, rich, slightly acid soil that is well drained. It does not grow well in hot, dry climates or in areas with warm winters. When plants become crowded, they should be divided.

Foamflower (*Tiarella cordifolia*)

Sometimes called False Mitrewort, Foamflower is a woodland perennial that spreads by rhizomes to form clumps of basal leaves. Mature plants are 6 inches high and as much as 2 feet across. The 4-inch-wide foliage is heart shaped and lobed or toothed. In the south, Foamflower is usually evergreen. Slender, 9-inch stems appear in mid-spring topped with 4-inch spikes of white, feathery, cylindrical flowers.

GROWING TIPS

Use Foamflower under trees and shrubs or in a border in partial shade. It will grow in dense shade, but will be more sparse in its growth. Foamflower grows best in cool, rich, acid soil that is moist and well drained. Once established, it will tolerate dry soil conditions. When clumps become crowded, they can be divided. Foamflower can also be grown from seeds.

Piggyback Plant *(Tolmiea menziesii)*

Zone 8

This plant got its unusual common name because it sprouts new plants at the base of the leaves where they join the stems, and they look like they are riding piggyback. It is also known as Mother-of-Thousands. The rich green, hairy leaves are heart shaped, 4 inches across, and either toothed or lobed. Greenish-white or reddish-brown flowers bloom in 8-inch spikes at the ends of 18- to 24-inch stems, but they are not showy.

GROWING TIPS

Partial to full shade and cool, moist soil are needed to grow Piggyback Plant. For optimum growth, the soil should also be rich, acid, and well drained. Apply a mulch to help keep the soil cool and moist during hot summers. To propagate Piggyback Plant, remove and root the new plantlets that form at the base of the leaves. You can also propagate it by division or from seeds.

American Barrenwort *(Vancouveria hexandra)* Zone 5

American Barrenwort is easily recognized by its wiry stems and its 3-leaflet leaves, which give it a dense, fernlike appearance. The dull green leaflets are heart shaped, lobed near the tip, and measure ½–1½ inches across. White, ⅓-inch flowers bloom in late spring in loose, airy, drooping panicles. American Barrenwort plants usually grow 4–8 inches high and spread by creeping roots to 24 inches across.

GROWING TIPS

American Barrenwort grows best in partial shade but will also grow in full shade. Plant it in rich, moist, well-drained soil and mulch it in summer to keep it cool. Divide American Barrenwort every 3–5 years to propagate new plants.

David Viburnum (*Viburnum davidii*)   Zone 8

David Viburnum is a handsome, compact, evergreen shrub that grows 1–2½ feet high and 4 feet wide. Its glossy, dark green leaves have 3 prominent veins that make them look like they are pleated. They are leathery and elliptical, measuring 3–6 inches long. The off-white, bell-shaped flowers bloom in flat, 2- to 3-inch clusters in summer but are not as showy as those of the larger viburnums. The flowers are followed by ornamental blue berries in fall that attract birds to the garden.

GROWING TIPS

David Viburnum prefers partial to full shade and moist, rich, slightly acid, well-drained soil. It benefits from a summer mulch, which keeps the roots cool, and needs protection from drying winds, especially in winter. In fall, decrease watering to allow the foliage to harden off before winter. Propagate new plants by layering or from cuttings or seeds.

Creeping Myrtle *(Vinca minor)*

Creeping Myrtle, also called Periwinkle, is an evergreen vine that forms a dense ground cover. One plant can reach 6–10 inches high and 24 inches across, rooting as it grows along the ground. Shiny, leathery, dark green leaves, which are 2 inches long, grow along thin stems. Flat, single flowers bloom in early spring to mid-spring. They are light to medium blue and ¾ inch across. The variety 'Alba' has white flowers and wider leaves; others have variegated leaves or double flowers. Big Periwinkle, *V. major,* is less hardy and has a more open habit.

Growing Tips
Creeping Myrtle will grow in a wide range of light conditions but grows best in partial to full shade, especially where summers are hot. It prefers a moderately fertile, well-drained soil. Give Creeping Myrtle an annual trimming to keep it neat and within bounds; mow it if necessary to encourage dense growth. When it becomes crowded, thin or divide it.

Horned Violet *(Viola cornuta)*

The flowers of Horned Violet range from white to yellow to apricot, red, and violet, and often have markings of a contrasting color in the center. The 5-petaled, 1½-inch flowers appear 1 to a stem, on flower stalks growing 5–8 inches high over tufted foliage. Horned Violets come into bloom in late spring; in cool climates, they will bloom all summer. Horned Violet plants spread and self-sow to form a dense, attractive ground cover.

GROWING TIPS

Horned Violets prefer a cool, humid climate. In hot areas, they will benefit from a summer mulch to keep the soil cool and moist but will not tolerate excessive heat. Plant them in partial to full shade and rich, moist, well-drained soil. Like other violets, Horned Violets grow well in shaded borders or under trees and shrubs. Divide the plants when they become crowded. You can also start new plants from seeds.

Sweet Violet (*Viola odorata*)

Sometimes called English Violet or Florists' Violet, Sweet Violet grows 4–8 inches high and spreads to 18–24 inches across. The plant sends out runners that root at their ends. The leaves, which are broadly heart shaped, are 3 inches or more across, growing in basal clumps. The 1-inch flowers are heavily and sweetly scented. They bloom in early spring, typically in shades of white, blue, or deep violet. The cultivar 'Royal Robe' has purple flowers; 'White Czar', pictured, is white; and 'Rosina' is pink.

Growing Tips

Grow Sweet Violets in partial shade, except where summer temperatures are high, in which case they prefer full shade. They like rich, moist, well-drained soil and benefit from a mulch to keep the soil cool. Mist the foliage regularly, especially on the undersides, to prevent spider mites. Sweet Violet plants can be propagated by division, by separation of rooted runners, or from seeds.

Woolly Blue Violet *(Viola sororia)*

Woolly Blue Violet grows 6 inches high and spreads to 18–24 inches across by stout creeping roots. The heart-shaped foliage, which may be smooth or hairy, reaches 6 inches across and forms clumps on long stalks. Half-inch, single flowers, which appear in early spring, are blue with a light center. This species is sometimes called Meadow Violet.

GROWING TIPS

Woolly Blue Violet prefers partial to full shade. Protection from the afternoon sun is a must. It grows best in rich, moist, well-drained soil; apply a mulch to keep it cool. To increase the plants, divide them or grow new plants from seeds. Woolly Blue Violet easily self-seeds, as do most violets, and can become invasive.

Barren Strawberry *(Waldsteinia ternata)*

B arren Strawberry forms an ever-green carpet 6 inches high. The glossy green leaves have 3 oval, lobed, 1- to 2-inch leaflets. Half-inch yellow flowers with prominent stamens bloom in small clusters on 8-inch stems in late spring. The fruit that follows the flowers resembles a strawberry but is dry, hairy, and inedible. Barren Strawberries spread by creeping roots but do not send out runners the way strawberries do. They are sometimes listed as *W. sibirica.*

Growing Tips

Barren Strawberry prefers partial shade. It grows best in soil that is rich and well drained, and it will tolerate dry soil if it is in a cool, shady spot. Divide Barren Strawberry when the plants become crowded.

Yellowroot (*Xanthorhiza simplicissima*)

This plant received its common name because the roots, as well as the bark, are yellow. Yellowroot is a deciduous, shrubby ground cover that spreads by underground stolons to 2 feet or more across. The foliage, which grows in whorls at the ends of 2-foot, upright stems, forms a dense mat. The leaves are oval, pointed, and deeply cut, resembling those of a fern. In the fall, the foliage turns yellow and then orange. Inconspicuous, brown to purple, ¼- to ½-inch flowers bloom in early spring in drooping clusters before the leaves open.

GROWING TIPS

Yellowroot is a perfect plant for shaded sites where soil drainage is poor, because it prefers heavy, very moist soil. New plants can be propagated by division or by planting root cuttings.

APPENDICES

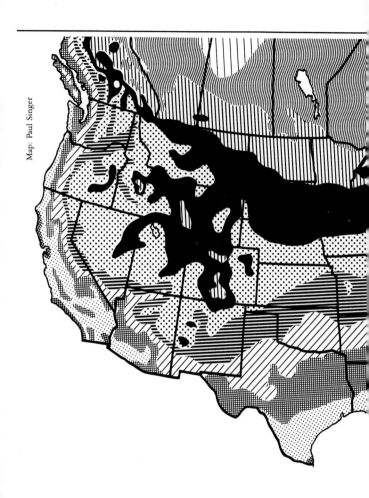

Map: Paul Singer

HARDINESS ZONE MAP

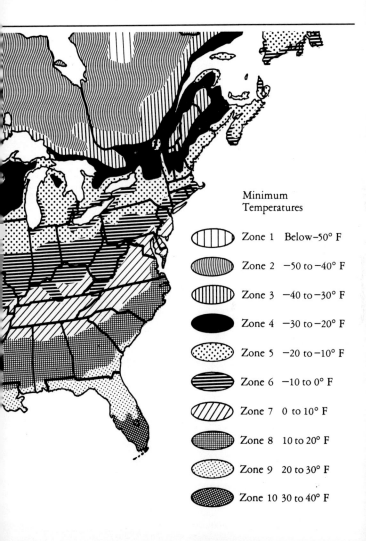

Minimum
Temperatures

Zone 1   Below −50° F

Zone 2   −50 to −40° F

Zone 3   −40 to −30° F

Zone 4   −30 to −20° F

Zone 5   −20 to −10° F

Zone 6   −10 to 0° F

Zone 7   0 to 10° F

Zone 8   10 to 20° F

Zone 9   20 to 30° F

Zone 10 30 to 40° F

GARDEN PESTS AND DISEASES

PLANT PESTS and diseases are a fact of life for a gardener. Therefore, it is helpful to become familiar with common pests and diseases in your area and to learn how to control them.

Symptoms of Plant Problems

Because the same general symptoms are associated with many diseases and pests, some experience is needed to determine their causes.

Diseases

Both fungi and bacteria are responsible for a variety of diseases ranging from leaf spots and wilts to root rot, but bacterial diseases usually make the affected plant tissues appear wetter than fungi do. Diseases caused by viruses and mycoplasma, often transmitted by aphids and leafhoppers, display such symptoms as mottled yellow or deformed leaves and twisted or stunted growth.

Insect Pests

Numerous insects attack plants. Sap-sucking insects—including aphids, leafhoppers, and scale insects—suck plant juices. The affected plant becomes yellow, stunted, and misshapen. Aphids and scale insects produce honeydew, a sticky substance that attracts ants and sooty mold fungus growth. Other pests with rasping-sucking mouthparts, such as thrips and spider mites, scrape plant tissue and then suck the juices that well up in the injured areas.

Leaf-chewers, namely beetles and caterpillars, consume plant leaves, whole or in part. Borers tunnel into shoots and stems, and their young larvae consume plant tissue, weakening the plant. Some insects, such as various grubs and maggots, feed on roots, weakening or killing the plant.

Nematodes

Microscopic roundworms called nematodes are other pests that attack roots and cause stunting and poor plant growth. Some kinds of nematodes produce galls on roots, while others produce them on leaves.

Environmental Stresses

Some types of plant illness result from environment-related stress, such as severe wind, drought, flooding, or extreme cold. Other problems are caused by salt toxicity, rodents, birds, nutritional deficiencies or excesses, pesticides, or damage from lawn mowers. Many of these injuries are avoidable if you take proper precautions.

Controlling Plant Problems

Always buy healthy disease- and insect-free plants, and select resistant varieties when available. Check leaves and stems for dead areas or off-color and stunted tissue. Later, when you plant your ground covers, be sure to prepare the soil properly.

Routine Preventives

By cultivating the soil routinely you will expose insects and disease-causing organisms to the sun and thus lessen their chances of surviving in your garden. In the fall be sure to destroy infested or diseased plants, remove dead leaves and flowers, and clean up plant debris. Do not add diseased or infested material to the compost pile. Spray plants with water from time to time to dislodge insect pests and remove suffocating dust. Pick off the larger insects by hand. To discourage fungal leaf spots and blights, always water plants in the morning and allow the leaves to dry off before nightfall. For the same reason, provide adequate air circulation around leaves and stems by spacing plants properly.

Weeds provide a home for insects and diseases, so pull them up or use pre-emergent herbicides (we do not recommend the use of any other type). If you use weed-killers on your lawn, do not apply them too close to ground covers or spray them on a windy day.

Insecticides and Fungicides

To protect plant tissue from injury due to insects and diseases, a number of insecticides and fungicides are available. However, few products control diseases due to bacteria, viruses, and mycoplasma. Pesticides are usually either "protectant" or "systemic" in nature. Protectants keep insects or disease organisms away from uninfected foliage, while systemics move through the plant and provide some therapeutic or eradicant action as well as protection. Botanical insecticides such as pyrethrum and rotenone have a shorter residual effect on pests, but are considered less toxic and generally safer for the user and the environment than inorganic chemical insecticides. Biological control through the use of organisms like *Bacillus thuringiensis* (a bacterium toxic to moth and butterfly larvae) is effective and safe.

Recommended pesticides may vary to some extent from region to region. Consult your local Cooperative Extension Service or plant professional regarding the appropriate material to use. Always check the pesticide label to be sure that it is registered for use on the pest and plant with which you are dealing. Follow the label concerning safety precautions, dosage, and frequency of application.

GLOSSARY

Acid soil
Soil with a pH value lower than 7.

Alkaline soil
Soil with a pH value of more than 7.

Annual
A plant whose entire life span, from sprouting to flowering and producing seeds, is encompassed in a single growing season.

Axil
The angle formed by a leafstalk and the stem from which it grows.

Basal leaf
A leaf at the base of a stem.

Biennial
A plant whose life span extends to two growing seasons, sprouting in the first growing season and then flowering, producing seed, and dying in the second.

Blade
The broad, flat part of a leaf.

Bract
A modified and often scalelike leaf, usually located at the base of a flower, a fruit, or a cluster of flowers or fruits.

Bud
A young and undeveloped leaf, flower, or shoot.

Bulb
A short underground stem, the swollen portion consisting mostly of fleshy, food-storing scale leaves.

Clasping
Surrounding or partly surrounding the stem, as in the base of the leaves of certain plants.

Compound
Similar parts aggregated into a whole, as in a compound leaf, composed of two or more leaflets.

Creeping
Prostrate or trailing over the ground or over other plants.

Cross-pollination
The transfer of pollen from one plant to another.

Crown
That part of a plant between the roots and the stem, usually at soil level.

Cultivar
An unvarying plant variety maintained by vegetative propagation rather than from seed.

Cutting
A piece of plant without roots; set in a rooting medium, it develops roots and is then potted as a new plant.

Deciduous
Dropping its leaves; not evergreen.

Dissected leaf
A deeply cut leaf; same as a divided leaf.

Division
Propagation of a plant by separating it into two or more pieces, each of which has at least one bud and some roots.

Double-flowered
Having more than the usual number of petals, usually arranged in extra rows.

Drooping
Pendant or hanging, as in the branches of a weeping willow.

Evergreen
Retaining green leaves on one year's growth until after the new leaves for the subsequent year have been formed.

Fertile
Bearing both stamens and pistils; able to produce seed.

Fruit
The fully developed ovary of a flower, containing seeds.

Genus
A group of closely related species; plural, genera.

Germinate
To sprout (applied to seeds).

Hardwood cutting
A cutting taken from a dormant plant after it has finished its yearly growth.

Heel
The base of a plant cutting or tuber used for propagation, often with some of the old stock attached.

Herbaceous perennial
A plant whose stems die back to ground level each fall, but that sends out new shoots and flowers for several successive years.

Horticulture
The cultivation of plants for ornament or food

Humus
Partly or wholly decomposed vegetable matter, an important constituent of garden soil.

Hybrid
The offspring of two parent plants that belong to different species, subspecies, genera, or varieties.

Invasive
Aggressively spreading from the original site of planting.

Irregular flower
A flower with petals that are not uniform in size or shape; such flowers are generally bilaterally symmetrical.

Lance shaped
Shaped like a lance; several times longer than wide, pointed at the tip and broadest near the base.

Layering
A method of propagation in which a stem is pegged to the ground and covered with soil and thus induced to send out roots.

Leaflet
One of the subdivisions of a compound leaf.

Leaf margin
The edge of a leaf.

Loam
A humus-rich soil containing up to 25 percent clay, up to 50 percent silt, and less than 50 percent sand.

Lobe
A segment of a cleft leaf or petal.

Lobed leaf
A leaf whose margin is shallowly divided.

Midrib
The primary rib or midvein of a leaf or leaflet.

Mulch
A protective covering spread over the soil around the base of plants to retard evaporation or control temperature.

Neutral soil
Soil that is neither acid nor alkaline, having a pH value of 7.

Node
The place on the stem where leaves or branches are attached.

Ovate
Oval, with the broader end at the base.

Panicle
An open flower cluster, blooming from bottom to top, and never terminating in a flower.

Peat moss
Partly decomposed moss, rich in nutrients and with a high water retention, used as a component of garden soil.

Perennial
A plant whose life span extends over several growing seasons and that produces seeds in several growing seasons.

Petal
One of a series of flower parts lying within the sepals and outside the stamens and pistils; often large and brightly colored.

pH
A symbol for the hydrogen ion content of the soil, and thus a means of expressing the acidity or alkalinity of the soil.

Pistil
The female reproductive organ of a flower.

Pollen
Minute grains containing the male germ cells and produced by the stamens.

Propagate
To produce new plants, either by vegetative means involving the rooting of pieces of a plant, or by sowing seeds.

Prostrate
Lying on the ground; creeping.

Raceme
A long flower cluster on which individual flowers each bloom on small stalks from a common, large, central stalk.

Regular flower
A flower with petals and sepals arranged around the center, like the spokes of a wheel; always radially symmetrical.

Rhizome
A horizontal stem at or just below the surface of the ground, distinguished from a root by the presence of nodes and often enlarged by food storage.

Rootstock
The swollen, more or less elongate, underground stem of a perennial herb; a rhizome.

Rosette
A crowded cluster of leaves; usually basal, circular, and at ground level.

Runner
A prostrate shoot, rooting at its nodes.

Seed
A fertilized, ripened ovule, naked in conifers but covered with a protective coating and contained in a fruit in all other garden plants.

Semievergreen
Retaining at least some green foliage well into winter, or shedding leaves only in cold climates.

Sepal
One of the outermost series of flower parts, arranged in a ring outside the petals, and usually green and leaflike.

Simple leaf
A leaf with an undivided blade; not compound or composed of leaflets.

Softwood
Green wood at an intermediate growth stage.

Solitary
Borne singly or alone; not in clusters.

Species
A population of plants or animals whose members are potentially able to breed with each other, and that is reproductively isolated from other populations.

Spike
An elongated flower cluster whose individual flowers lack stalks.

Spine
A strong, sharp, usually woody projection from the stem or branches of a plant.

Stamen
The male reproductive organ of a flower.

Sterile
Lacking stamens or pistils and therefore unable to produce seeds.

Stolon
A horizontal stem, just above or beneath the soil, from the tip of which a new plant arises; a runner.

Stratify
To keep seeds under cool, dark, moist conditions to encourage them to break dormancy and germinate after treatment.

Subshrub
A partly woody plant.

Subspecies
A naturally occurring geographical variant of a species.

Succulent
A plant with thick, fleshy leaves or stems that contain abundant water-storage tissue. Cacti and stonecrops are examples.

Taproot
The main, central root of a plant.

Terminal
Borne at the tip of a stem or shoot, rather than in the axil.

Toothed
Having the margin shallowly divided into small, toothlike segments.

Tuber
A swollen, mostly underground stem that bears buds and serves as a storage site for food.

Variegated
Marked, striped, or blotched with some color other than green.

Variety
A population of plants that differs consistently from the typical form of the species, occurring naturally in a geographical area. Also applied, incorrectly but popularly, to forms produced in cultivation.

Vegetative propagation
Propagation by means other than seed.

Whorl
A group of three or more leaves or shoots that emerge from a stem at a single node.

PHOTO CREDITS

INDEX

CHANTICLEER PRESS
STEWART, TABORI & CHANG

Publisher
ANDREW STEWART

Senior Editor
ANN WHITMAN

Editor
CAROL MCKEOWN

Project Editor
AMY HUGHES

Production
KATHY ROSENBLOOM
KARYN SLUTSKY

Design
JOSEPH RUTT